T0147441

Music

and

Human
Health

Jin H Wang

iUniverse, Inc.
New York Bloomington

Music and Human Health

iUniverse books may be ordered through booksellers or by contacting:

iUniverse
1663 Liberty Drive
Bloomington, IN 47403
www.iuniverse.com
1-800-Authors (1-800-288-4677)

Because of the dynamic nature of the Internet, any Web addresses or links contained in this book may have changed since publication and may no longer be valid. The views expressed in this work are solely those of the author and do not necessarily reflect the views of the publisher, and the publisher hereby disclaims any responsibility for them.

ISBN: 978-1-4502-2845-9 (sc)
ISBN: 978-1-4502-2846-6 (ebook)

Library of Congress Control Number: 2010905860

Printed in the United States of America

iUniverse rev. date: 04/30/2010

Contents

Preface

Sarah McLachlan is one of the world's best singers, songwriters, and artists. Winner of three Grammys and eight Juno awards, she is the founder of the Lilith Fair tour (1997–1999), the largest all-female musician music festival in history. The Lilith Fair tour will return thirty-six large cities in North American and Europe. Her new music video, "One Dream" was featured on NBC on January 24, 2010. She performed her "Ordinary Miricle" on 2010 Winter Olympic Games Opening Ceremony on Feburary 12 and her "Angel" on ABC Jimmy Kimmel Live on March 25. ABC will provide reports about the tour in the summer.

I believe that music and medicine are critical to human health. We know we need medicine in our daily life. However, I believe that we need music in our daily life too. Music, including Sarah's songs, brings joy and peace to people. Sarah's beautiful songs reach deep into the heart and soul, inspiring, bringing happiness, comforting, and helping people through hard times.

Introduction

Human health can be divided into body health and soul health. Medicine has played a significant role in the maintenance of body health. There are many examples of medical care in our daily life: taking care of wounds, fractures, cuts, and bacterial infection with antibiotics; preventing many viral infections and a few bacterial infections with vaccines; treating diseases that result from a lack of certain proteins or hormones with replacement therapies, such as insulin, growth hormones, and enzymes; treating viral infections with several antiviral drugs or interferons; transplanting bone marrow or organs; and developing diagnosis techniques, such as blood, urine, tissue testing, X-ray, CT, and MRI examinations.

One significant contribution to the increased longevity is the reduction of death caused by infections, especially childhood infections. The incidence of death caused by heart diseases has also been reduced in recent years due to advancements in prevention and treatment. However, advancements in behavioral sciences, or the health of the soul, have been more limited. The mechanisms of actions of many drugs in this field are not fully understood. In addition, most drugs of this class have certain adverse effects. More challenging is what to do with people that are moderately depressed, having difficult times due to loss of a significant other, or have just experienced a trauma event, such as giving birth to a child.

In this book, we are going to talk about medicine, human health, and music (especially the music of Sarah McLachlan) and its role in the life of people and their happiness.

The unique voice of Sarah McLachlan and her songs are deeply loved and appreciated by her fans. Comments from her fans indicate that her music not only made people feel better, happy, and inspired but helped them overcome difficult times and sad moments; in some cases, her songs even saved lives. Music has also improved the life of seniors and patients with heart disease and cancer.

The book is full of facts, useful information, lovely poems, and stories. The intent of this book is to introduce the important role of music in lives of people, and in the promotion of human health. I hope that music is part of your life and also a part of your health.

Chapter 1: Music

Music is an art form whose medium is sound. Common elements of music are pitch, rhythm, dynamics, and the sonic qualities of timbre and texture. The word "music" originated from Greek word μουσική (*mousike*). Music can be divided into genres, such as Pop, Rock, Country, Classic, Jazz, Alternate.

Music is usually pleasant to listen to. Music that is favored in certain special periods may not be appreciated other times. Music good for one society might not be really welcomed in others. Songs, comparing to instrumental music, even have more limitations, namely language meaning that some music is appreciated only in a given historical time or by a special society. However, one might argue that any sound is music. To some degree, this is true. The blowing wind, a rushing stream, singing frogs, the voice of bird, the prolonged shrill sound of the male cicada, the speech or talk of human beings, even a distant thunderstorm are all music in a way. However, an intolerable sound is noise, not music. Even more, when certain limits are passed, noise is not only unpleasant but also harmful.

This book is more focused on recent music, with an

emphasis on singers that have made a great impact in the twentieth and twenty-first centuries. It is not a music textbook, and the author apologizes if he has failed to include your favored musicians or singers due to the limit of the book.

Classical music (1750–1800) features composers such as Joseph Haydn and Wolfgang Amadeus Mozart. Their music is often homophonic, with a prominent voice-like melody. There are three major forms of popular instrumental music today: the sonata, the concerto, and the symphony. During 1800s, the so-called Romantic was led by transitional composers Ludwig van Beethoven and Franz Schubert.

The first opera was written during the Baroque period (1600–1750). The future of opera is challenging. The strength of opera, a beautiful singing language, might also be its limitation. Singing in English while keeping an operatic like voice, demonstrated by Kiri Te Kanawa, Sarah Brightman, and some new faces like Jessica Stecklein, might be of interest. The excellent singing of "You'll Never Walk Alone" by the celebrated Three Tenors also indicated the value of opera singers in the more popular modern languages, which might just offer the opportunity to keep opera in its original forms.

Church music, which can be traced back to the mediaeval era (500–1400) is some not only in churches but also in society groups, such as by chamber singers. The melody of church music is usually simple, but beautiful, and can be easily followed by almost everyone. Whether church music should be called heaven music is an interesting question.

American Music (1866–present): Broadway and Pop

From the first crude but popular musical theater show The Black Crook in 1866, American music has been rich and colorful. George M. Cohan in the early twentieth century created very personalized show characters and songs that had strong purpose, as seen in his first hit show *Little Johnny Jones*. George Gershwin, the musical soul of 1920s, introduced jazz to Broadway and wrote *Swanee*, an international hit song. The 1950s were the Golden Years of musical theater. Classical musicals included *West Side Story*, *The Sound of Music*, *My Fair Lady*, *The King and I*, and *The Music Man*. *West Side Story* featured a great song, "Somewhere." In the 1960s, rock and roll reached Broadway.

Pop is a revolution in the history of music. Pop king Elvis Presley (1935–1977) was a dominant figure of twentieth century. Pop music composition is less restricted, easy to sing, and sometimes a song consists of singing and talking. Some of his songs, such as "Good Luck Charm," "Can't Help Falling In Love," and "Love Me Tender," are still popular today. The Beatles and The Rolling Stones were very popular in the sixties and are still favored by youth. Another figure from this century is Andy Williams (1927–present). His famous songs include "Moon River," "Autumn Leaves," "Love Story," and "Can't Take My Eyes Off of You." Amazingly, when he was past the age of eighty, he still sang "Moon River" with its dramatic tenor ending. His story of how to keep life and music going for more than sixty years will be really interesting and helpful for all young singers. Other pop singers, such as Michael Jackson, Billy Joel, Josh Groban, Bryan Adams, Michael Bublé, and Andrea Bocelli, are great as well.

There have been many great female singers as well. Barbra Streisand is one of the most famous sopranos of the twentieth century. Celine Dion was famous overnight for her beautiful singing of "My Heart Will Go On" in the film *Titanic*.

The great performance of a special wind music instrument supported her vocal really well.

This book focuses on one of the world's best singers, Sarah McLachlan, as well as her contribution to human history. Newcomers like Taylor Swift and other new faces in Lilith Tour 2010 are very popular too.

Favored Chinese Music

Before we talk more about Sarah, I would like to give you a brief overview of some of my favorite Chinese singers. Music in China has long history of over three thousand years. In China, there are many great folk songs. One song that I like a lot is "Zai Na Yao Yuan De Di Fang," or "At a Remote Place," made famous by several famous male singers, like Song-Hua Hu, Lang Dao, and Da-Wei Jiang. "Man Shan Hong Yi Shi Chai Xia," or "Red Leaves over Mountains Seem Like Colorful Cloud," was sung by a great female singer Min-Yin Zhu in the seventies. It was in a movie and I was really impressed by its beautiful melody and dynamic.

Teresa Teng (1953–1995), from Taiwan, was the best pop singer in China. She was introduced into my life as a cultural example of capitalism by a party member during a meeting in 1979. During the meeting, "bad" examples of her music on tape sounded great to me, and I found myself wanting more of these "bad" samples. Since 1980, Teng has been one of the most popular female singers in China. Her voice was very good and her singing made you felt close and relaxed. Her signature songs include "Moon Represents My Heart," "When You Will Come Again," and "Little Town Stories."

Gu-YI Li, Li-Yuan Peng, Zu-Ying Shong, A-Min Mao, and Na Li are among the top female singers. Top male singers include Huan Liu, Xiang Fei, and so on.

There are several great Chinese singers in the United States, such as Hao-Jian Tian, Hai-Tao Bai, and Ling-Ling He, and Hong-Fa Chu.

Sarah McLachlan and Lilith Fair

Lilith Fair, the biggest female music festival in history, was founded by Sarah in 1997. During the three years of the Lilith Fair tour, Sarah was everywhere. Now she is bringing back Lilith Tour this summer in cities all over the world. She also has a new album, *The Laws of Illusion*, scheduled to hit stores on June 15, 2010. You can preorder it from her Web site, www.sarahmclachlan.com

Her professional and her personal life, including a new lovely story full of music that creates the first conceptual fusion between music and medicine, will be discussed in detail. It is my hope that this book will open the era of the practical application of music in the enhancement of public health and human wellness.

Chapter 2: Sarah McLachlan

Snapshot

Name	Sarah McLachlan (Sarah Ann McLachlan)
Height	5' 7" (170 cm)
Date of Birth	January 28, 1968
Birthplace	Halifax, Nova Scotia, Canada
Star sign	Aquarius
Nationality	Canadian
Ethnicity	White
High School	Queen Elizabeth High School, Halifax, Nova Scotia, Canada
University	Nova Scotia College of Art and Design
Occupation	Musician
Claim to Fame	*Fumbling towards Ecstasy*
1st Album	*Touch*, 1988
Best selling album	*Surfacing*, sold over 11 million copies. Billboard #1 in 1998
Signature songs	"Angel," "I Will Remember You," "Adia," "Building a Mystery"
Grammy Awards	3
Juno Awards	8
Albums sold	Over 40 million

Sarah McLachlan was born on January 28, 1968, and

adopted in Halifax, Nova Scotia. Her adoptive mother and father raised her in an average middle-income family. She has two older brothers. Both her mother and father provided Sarah their best support. She married her drummer, Ashwin Sood, in 1997 and gave birth to two daughters, India Ann Sushil Sood, on April 6, 2002, and Taja (the Hindi word for "crown") Summer Sood, on June 24, 2007, both in Vancouver. McLachlan announced her separation from Ashwin Sood in September 2008. Her mother died of cancer in 2001. Her father, Dr. Jack McLachlan, is a retired biologist.

Sarah McLachlan is a very sophisticated singer, with a folksy look and a nature-loving aura. Sarah is an accomplished and successful musician, one of the best in the world.

Music Career of Sarah McLachlan

Sarah McLachlan is one of the most famous female singers originating from Canada. Every Sarah song is an escapade into a fantasy world due to her sensual voice and natural elegance. Sarah is also one of the nicest artists in the world, with a warmth and soft character. She was born in Halifax, Nova Scotia on January 28, 1968. She started to sing at age four. Sarah had training in piano and guitar during her school years. She also took singing lessons regularly. At age seventeen, she was offered a record contract by Nettwerk Productions. Although very interested in the contract, Sarah, on the advice of her parents, decided to study at the Nova Scotia College of Art and Design. When Nettwerk called again, she signed a deal with the label on October 2, 1987. After singing with Nettwerk, Sarah moved to Vancouver, British Columbia. All her albums are certified gold, platinum, or multi-platinum by the RIAA. *Touch* (1988) and *Solace*

(1991) were both gold sellers. Pierre Marhand is the producer of all her albums except *Touch*.

Her 1994 breakthrough *Fumbling towards Ecstasy* reached 3X-platinum. Sarah's landmark fifth album, the 10X-platinum (or diamond) *Surfacing* (1997) contained two Grammy Award-winning tracks: "Building a Mystery" won for Best Female Pop Vocal and "Last Dance" was voted Best Pop Instrumental. In 1998, the soundtrack of the Wim Wenders film *City of Angels* reached number one on the Billboard chart, featuring the Sarah McLachlan track *Angel*.

In 1999, Sarah's 4X-platinum album *Mirrorball* earned Sarah her third Grammy Award for Best Female Pop Vocal (1999, for the track "I Will Remember You").

In 2003, *Afterglow*, a 2X-platinum album, was released and received two Grammy Award nominations: Best Pop Vocal Album and Best Female Pop Vocal (for "Fallen").

In 2004, her high-profile video "World on Fire," directed by Sophie Muller, was released and had a big social impact. Jon Pareles commented in the *New York Times* "a modestly brilliant gesture: it stacks up budget items for a typical clip against what the same $150,000 budget would buy as relief efforts—cattle, bicycles, housing, education, medicine..." "World on Fire" earned a Grammy nomination for Best Short Form Music Video. The $150,000 video budget was distributed among eleven charitable organizations around the world (except $15 for a Sony mini DV tape).

Sarah McLachlan's *Afterglow* tour included many cities in United States, Australia, and Canada and was performed at a May 24, 2005, concert at New York's Madison Square Garden.

In October 2006, Sarah released *Wintersong*, her first album of holiday-themed songs. Among the highlights:

"Happy Xmas (War Is Over)" by John Lennon and Yoko Ono, "River" by Joni Mitchell, and all-time seasonal favorites "I'll Be Home For Christmas" and "Have Yourself a Merry Little Christmas." The platinum-selling *Wintersong* reached number seven on the Billboard chart. The disc was nominated for a Grammy Award for Best Traditional Pop Vocal Album.

Sarah's many cover songs and collaborations formed the repertoire for *Rarities, B-Sides and Other Stuff Volume 2*, released April 29, 2008.

For more information, please go to www.myspace.com/sarahmclachlan.

Milestones

- Sarah McLachlan has sold over 40 million recordings worldwide since her recording career began in 1988.
- Sarah is a three-time Grammy Award winner:
- "I Will Remember You" – Best Female Pop Vocal Performance
  - "Last Dance" – Best Pop Instrumental Performance
  - "Building a Mystery" – Best Female Pop Vocal Performance
- Sarah has received 21 Juno Award nominations.
- Lilith Fair, a touring festival of all-female artists, founded by Sarah McLachlan, brought together two million people over its three-year history (1997–1999) and raised millions for charities.
- *Rolling Stone, Time,* and *Entertainment Weekly* all published cover stories about Sarah McLachlan.

- Sarah McLachlan is one of awardees of the Elizabeth Cady Stanton Visionary Award for her contribution in advancing the careers of female artists.
- In 2003, Sarah McLachlan founded the Sarah McLachlan Music Outreach Program, which has provided free music education classes to many Vancouver inner city youths.
- Lilith Fair tour cities and artists have been announced and the tour will begin in June 27, 2010.
- Sarah is a singer, a songwriter, a composer, a pianist, and a guitar player, a talent seldom seen in music history.

Sarah's Songs

Strong personal and emotional experience is embedded in almost all her songs and in her poem-like lyrics. This is because, as opposed to most singers, Sarah writes all her lyrics. Her personal signature in her songs are lively and loved by audience. As a big fan of her commented on her Facebook page, instrumental music is the green leaves (of a flower) that enhance her vocal expressions. Her lyrics are the poems of the heart. Her beautiful voice touches the soul. The combination of these three in a creative way, as Sarah always does, produces a beautiful piece of music. In short, Sarah's songs fill our hearts and touch our soul. Although "Angel" is her signature song, she has multiple recognizable hits, like "Adia," "I Will Remember You," "World On Fire," "Fallen," "U Want Me 2," "Building a Mystery," and "Good Enough."

"Angel" and *Surfacing*

In 1997, Sarah released *Surfacing*, her best-selling album, which earned two Grammy Awards and four Juno Awards. So far the album has sold over 11 million copies worldwide, with great international success. The fatal overdose of Jonathan Melvoin, a touring keyboardist, inspired her to write *Angel*, a song featured in *City of Angels*, a motion picture released in early 1998. *Surfacing* reached number one on the Billboard chart the same year.

"Angel" is a beautiful song. The first time when I listened to it I was completely attracted by it and have been a fan of Sarah since.

Fumbling towards Ecstasy

In 1993, Sarah visited several places around the world, including Cambodia. There she saw the poor living conditions and met a twelve-year-old girl who was HIV positive . She was shocked and felt that she wanted to help poor people all over the world. This passion led her to compose songs for *Fumbling towards Ecstasy*.

World On Fire and Care of the World

Sarah McLachlan toured with her 2003 album release, *Afterglow*, which contained the singles "Fallen," "Stupid," and "World On Fire." "World On Fire," a socially conscious video, explains how it would benefit the communities around the world that received the $150,000 planned budget for the video that Sarah donated.

Sarah McLachlan took part in a tsunami disaster relief telethon on NBC in early 2005. She also joined Delerium live on stage for their first-ever performance of "Silence." The concert was titled One World: The Concert for Tsunami Relief and raised approximately $3.6 million for disaster relief.

Sarah has supported the ASPCA and animal welfare,

raising $30 million for the ASPCA since her song "Angel" was featured in ASPCA ads in 2006.

In 2005, McLachlan performed her hit "Angel" with Josh Groban for the Philadelphia installment of the Live 8 concerts, held in nine major cities around the world and coinciding with the G8 summit to fight poverty in Africa by cancelling debt.

Wintersong

In 2006, Sarah released her first holiday themed-album, *Wintersong.* The album includes very popular songs like "Silent Night," "O Little Town of Bethlehem," "Christmas Time Is Here," and "Have Yourself a Merry Little Christmas." She recorded John Lennon's "Happy Xmas (War Is Over)" with her outreach children and youth choir. The album featured her own track, "Wintersong," as the title. The album has peaked at number seven on the Billboard 200 and has been certified platinum in United States.

Wintersong was nominated for both a Grammy Award and a Juno Award.

Sarah McLachlan's Music Outreach is a free music program offered in Vancouver's inner city. The program provides high-quality instruction in guitar, piano, percussion, and choir and helps youth develop a lifelong love of music, as well as enthusiasm for learning and a positive attitude about their abilities. It is a place for young people to explore their creative potential in music that will inspire them to succeed in life.

O Little Town of Bethlehem
Traditional

O little town of Bethlehem
How still we see thee lie
Above thy deep and dreamless sleep
The silent stars go by
Yet in thy dark streets shineth
The everlasting Light
The hopes and fears of all the years
Are met in thee tonight

For Christ is born of Mary
And gathered all above
While mortals sleep, the angels keep
Their watch of wondering love
O morning stars together
Proclaim the holy birth
And praises sing to God the King
And Peace to men on earth

How silently, how silently
The wondrous gift is given!
So God imparts to human hearts
The blessings of His heaven.
No ear may his His coming,
But in this world of sin,
Where meek souls will receive him still,
The dear Christ enters in.

O holy Child of Bethlehem
Descend to us, we pray
Cast out our sin and enter in
Be born to us today
We hear the Christmas angels
The great glad tidings tell
O come to us, abide with us
Our Lord Emmanuel

Silent Night lyric
Traditional

Silent night, holy night
All is calm, all is bright
Round yon Virgin Mother and Child
Holy Infant so tender and mild
Sleep in heavenly peace
Sleep in heavenly peace

Silent night, holy night!
Shepherds quake at the sight
Glories stream from heaven afar
Heavenly hosts sing Alleluia!
Christ, the Saviour is born
Christ, the Saviour is born

Silent night, holy night
Son of God, love's pure light
Radiant beams from Thy holy face
With the dawn of redeeming grace
Jesus, Lord, at Thy birth
Jesus, Lord, at Thy birth

One Dream

I love music, Chinese chess, Go, and dancing. I especially love the game of Go. Go originated in China, and it is popular in China, Taiwan, Japan, and Korea. The standard format is 19 x 19. You can play first with 9 x 9, then 13 x 13. It usually takes about three hours to play one 19 x 19 game. If timed, it may take one and a half hours. During some weekends in the early eighties I would play several games a day. I believe that it really makes people think. The object is not to kill the opponent but rather to coexist, then win or lose a little bit. Huge wins and losses do not make the game interesting at all. Now there is a Go Congress in the United States every year. When a better player plays with a weaker player, the latter is allowed to play up to nine stones on the board first, making the game more challenging for the better player.

I love music. I can dance with music and feel good listening to the rhythm. I like many songs, but there are only a few I can listen to multiple times, including some Chinese folk songs, some songs by Tseng, songs from *The Sound of Music*, and Mozart concertos for flute and orchestra that I bought in the early nineties which are still in perfect condition. One song that I really enjoyed to listen to is a song called "Red Leaves over the Mountains Seem Like Colorful Cloud" from an old seventies Chinese move. It was sung by Min-Ying Zu.

I first heard Sarah several years ago. I was immediately attracted to her music. Unfortunately, I only understood a few words, but I was captured by the voice, that a voice that was not only beautiful and lovely but which played with my soul. Thanks to God, the radio told me it was "Angel" by Sarah McLachlan. I said to myself, "That is enough." I went to a nearby Best Buy store. In the CD section, it took me quite a while to find her albums, as the CDs were not alphabetized in that store. Finally I found her. There were a few of her CDs. I selected *Afterglow Live*. It has a DVD in addition to a CD. I watched the whole show non-stop. Sorry, my dear Sarah, I understood all your talks, such as "Like to extract blood from stone", "30 seconds dead space." But I had a hard time understanding some songs. However, I was completely attracted to the show, by her beautiful singing. As many fans have commented, it is her voice that is so beautiful. The DVD did provide lyrics. I said to myself that I can enjoy listening to her singing and I don't care what she is singing about now, because I know I will definitely listen again and again. I try to understand by listening time after time and enjoy it even more as new experience, although sometimes I did peek at the lyrics.

My attention then went to her. She is so beautiful. Her drummer, who eventually became her husband, is also a great performer. She was very happy to be a mom. She has even said that the baby, not her music, is number one for her now. She created a special song for her dear husband. I felt really happy for her.

Then something changed. The news came that she had separated from her husband. I was kind of surprised. Following this the song "U Want Me 2" came out.

I was captivated by the beauty and the deep sadness of the song and the video performance. I wondered what might happen so they separated. I thought I should call her and talk to her as a man, a friend. I tried to e-mail her. Believe or not, man may make mistakes for some reasons, but they usually still love their family, especially when children are involved. I felt that way because I am a man.

In the meantime, I listened to her music a lot more, and it has become part of my life.

In October 2009, I got an e-mail from her regarding the release of a new single, "One Dream." I loved it. Believe it or not, I understood the meanings of her lyrics much more this time. I loved the music, the vocals, and the sentiment. Another thing I felt was that she was more attractive to me. I felt her "One Dream" photo told a lot more about her and her change. I felt I should try to help her. Usually I am pretty quiet—I just listen and watch—but this time I decided to write a comment she and others could see. I am not sure I can give her the "courage" she is looking for, but I thought I might be able to let her feel better. Here is the comment that I posted on her One Dream Facebook:

> So beautiful and so lovely, Sarah!!! Thank you for all your songs, great gifts for all from angel. We all do our best!!!

There were a lot of very good comments, such as "Absolutely beautiful!" and "Fab Voice!" Those fans expressed strong love for her songs and for her. Some try to offer their help to the tour. Interestingly, a comment right after my comment was "Please consider marrying me!" I thought "Okay, as a single now, I'll be happy to." Well, it was just a thought that time. Days later, I put in another comment:

> Angel was the first song I heard on the radio. I love all your songs, Sarah. *Afterglow Live* is my best gift to my friends and relatives during the holiday season. Wish you have great success on your EU tour and US tour.

I was stating a fact, but actually I was trying to suggest that all fans could "spread" Sarah's good music and songs to their dear ones. Now I understood why brothers and sisters in churches try so hard to get new people to go to their churches, because they do believe it. One day I went onto her MySpace page. I was totally attracted by her videos. I just listened and watched her during each night, up to 2 a.m. on Friday and Saturday night. I was really becoming more attracted to her. I read all the comments posted on her Facebook page. One thing was very clear to me: many more people needed her. When they were in a normal mood, they felt better. When they were sad, when they were alone, when they were driving long distances, it was Sarah's songs that helped them through the difficult times.

Here are some summarized comments from Sarah's Facebook:

- One fan stated that Sarah McLachlan was her absolute favorite singer in the world and inspired her so much. Sarah is an angel and heals the world with her soul and songs. She is dying to meet Sarah, for Sarah's music heals her and opens up her heart to the world.
- Another fan commented that Sarah has the most beautiful voice he has ever heard and Sarah's lyrics go deep into his heart and soul.
- Another fan stated that Sarah sings like no other! She inspires us with the beauty and humanity of her voice and spirit. "One Dream" has put a peaceful smile on her face amidst all the chaos in her life.

In the meantime, I also felt that her video had a big impact on me. I never saw her, and never talked to her, but I felt an even stronger desire that I wanted to help her, I wanted to help a helper, within my ability. I did not realize that I might be falling for her after I listened to "Angel" and watched *Afterglow Live* (show, videos, and backstage) the first time, but at that time I was more like a friend lover. So I wrote another comment in lyric format. Here is it:

> You're just too great to be true.
> Can't take my eyes and ears off you.
> It's a wonderful news U'll be DC and other cities.
> People here and there are waiting for U.
> All want U want me 2.
> Captured by the beauty and deep sadness.
> It will be so fortunate to see and listen to Angel.
> It's a splendored thing a real Angel's with us.
> All hearts'll be filled with Angel songs.
>
> The current city list for the Lilith Fair tour is out, and you can check it out at Sarah's MySpace webpage. If you are lucky and happen to be in one of the cities selected, please think about what you can do for the tour, at least in your city.

I tried is to express the feelings of myself and all other fans. I encourage all fans to think about ways to further support Sarah and her tour.

The above comment highlighted my feeling or love to Sarah's music. I really enjoy listening to her music, like when

I drive. However, I get more out of watching her than just listening to her. I really appreciate her effort to express her songs in video format. Another thing might be that I can't see her, so I just watch her video. You know what man is doing. I am a man and I thought if I can meet her it will be great.

Interestingly, the next comment is

"☺☺☺☺☺☺☺♫ I missed you"

No name "to" and no "from." I thought it might be another fan. I did have a slight feeling that it could be Sarah in responding to my comment. Indeed, when I look back now it is actually a statement of true love about her music from my heart.

One day I had a thought, and I wished one day someone could compose it into a song for Sarah. I called it "Sarah."

Here is the first draft of the lyrics:

Sarah

You're just too great to be true.
Can't keep my eyes and ears off you.
It's so wonderful U'll be cities around the world.
People here and there are waiting for U.
All want U want me 2.
Captured by the beauty and deep sadness.

It'll be so fortunate to see and listen to Angel.
At the joyful times
During the sad or difficult moments.
It's a splendored thing a real Angel's with us.

Bring peace and joy to every one.
All hearts'll be filled with Angel songs.

To make it easier to compose, I revised the lyrics. Here is the version I posted on her "One Dream" Facebook site.

> Sarah, I made some changes of the first draft so it might be loved by all current fans and future fans, no matter male or female. More need to be done.

Sarah

> You're just too great to be true.
> Can't keep my eyes and ears off you.
> So wonderful U'll be cities around the world.
> People here and there are waiting for U.
> All want U want me 2.
> Every mind'll be amazed by lovely you.
>
> You're just too beautiful to be real.
> Can't help to see and listen to you.
> No matter at joyful times or sad moments.
> It's a splendored thing a real Angel's with us.
> Bring peace and joy to everyone.
> All hearts'll be filled with Angel songs.
>
> Have a happy Friday night and weekend!
>
> J

At the same time, I sent a comment to all the fans:

Hi, all Sarah fans,

I wrote down my feelings for Sarah and her songs. I hope you like it to be a lyric for a song. Any suggestions are welcome. I wish it will be one of your songs one day, a song for our Sarah. I am not an artist or a musician, but I wish we can have a song for our beautiful and lovely Sarah, a song we can sing for her.

Any suggestions or comments?

J

Then things changed. No new comments were coming in. I was the only one really commenting. I said to myself that no matter what I will keep it going, and I am happy to keep it going unless Sarah decides to close it. I thought it was good for her, good for the tour, and good for other people.

Quiz

To have fun, I added a quiz one day:

Best Titles from a Great Poet of Our Time

Please identify who the poet and all the titles of her poems below. They are great gifts for you and your family members during the holidays. They are available at www.sarahmclachlan. com.

Adia, Hold On
Please Don't Give Up On Us

A Ben's Song Is Good Enough
We"re All Drawn To The Rhythm

Angel, Please Wait
I've Fallen as a Sweet Surrender
I Will Remember You
Even on the Path of Thorns
Time after Time We'll Be Fumbling towards
Ecstasy

World on Fire
No Fear, Get Water from River Elsewhere
We Need Plenty Ice Too
I Will Not Forget You, Ice Cream
Push All into the Fire
It Is an Ordinary Miracle

We Wouldn't Be Homeless

Answers

Adia, Hold On
Please Don't Give Up on Us
A Ben's Song *is* Good Enough
We're all Drawn to the Rhythm

Angel, *please* Wait
I've Fallen *as a* Sweet Surrender
I Will Remember You
Even on the Path of Thorns
Time after Time *we'll be* Fumbling towards
Ecstasy

World On Fire
No Fear, *get water from* River Elsewhere
We need Plenty Ice *too*
I Will Not Forget You, Ice Cream
Push *all* into the Fire
It is an Ordinary Miracle
We wouldn't be Homeless

Please note the following titles:

Plenty
Ice
River
Elsewhere

Thanksgiving

I thought if I introduced some interesting topics, fans might make comments, so I introduced the topic of Music and Happiness.

Music and Happiness

Beautiful music and beautiful voice. It is so great and I can't help to introduce a series of short discussions about music in our life. Thanksgiving is a big holiday for many people each year. Families get together, eat delicious food, talk to each other, then many will turn on music. Even more, some will sing, others will dance with music. There are many great holiday songs, like "Happy Xmas—Wintersong." Really to me, holidays without friends, family members, relatives, and music would not be a happy holiday.

Happy Thanksgiving to Sarah and everyone!

I went on with:

> Well, many things are important to humans. We need air, water, food and we need friends, family, etc. One thing, among others, that is essential to me is listening to music, especially Sarah's beautiful songs. Many fans have the same feelings. When they drive along, when they feel sad and unhappy, it is Sarah's songs with them. Believe it or not, magic is magic. When Sarah was sad, I felt sad too. When she was happy, I also felt happy.

> Sarah, wish you and your daughters a very happy Thanksgiving!

The next comment was

> For lack of a better comment, I'll quote Stevie Nicks: "Sarah, you're the poet of my heart." There has never been anyone who can write songs to express everything that I long to express. Great job.

> It was November 25, 2009. World AIDS Day was December 1. I thought a lot more about what should be done and could be done while enjoying the beautiful music on DC's Magic

FM 95.7. I wrote a poem about AIDS, wishing it would be composed into a simple song one day. I thought about Sarah's "World On Fire" and the attention she gives to the AIDS crisis, so I posted my thoughts on her Facebook page.

Here is the message I posted, on November 30, 2009:

> As you know, tomorrow will be World AIDS DAY (December 1). Here is a draft. Hopefully you will like the wording.

> Sarah, I know you are really busy. If you like to consider it, it is all in your hands. It seems to me both you and our youth like the Beatles.

> **A Rubber Thing**

> 15, 16, 18
> Golden time to learn
> Girls are singing
> Boys are playing
> What a wonderful life

> 16, 17, 18
> Miserable time to regret
> Girls are crying
> Boys are yelling
> Forgot a rubber thing

> HIV, AIDS, AIDS
> A lifelong disease
> Girls, prevention

Boys, prevention
Don't forget the rubber thing

After posted this comment, I looked again the comments before Thanksgiving. Suddenly it occurred to me that no one else can write that comment except Sarah herself.

> For lack of a better comment, I'll quote Stevie Nicks: "Sarah, you're the poet of my heart." There has never been anyone who can write songs to express everything that I long to express. Great job.

I was thrilled. I replied to her immediately with a bit of hesitation. I sent an e-mail to Sarah in early December 2009:

> My dear, you have a big tender heart.
>
> I usually pay more attention to today, tomorrow, and the future. History usually does not weigh too much on me. But when I watch more about you, the more I feel your tender heart. I'll give you a big hug.
>
> I understood the impact of this epidemic on you. Real life experience usually has big impact on people. One of my colleagues came back from a meeting in Africa and told me that there if you shake hands with four people, there is one positive for HIV-1. That is 25%. Luckily the epidemic is under control in more developed countries. Current treatments are effective,

but they have some side effects. Once a patient stated on TV that she had a big lump (fat) on her neck, which was caused by anti-HIV drugs, but would not still alive without the drugs.

To me, before we have a treatment that can clear out the virus from the body, the best approach is prevention. We need an effective vaccine. However, from preclinical to final approval it will take at least 10 years if you have a good vaccine candidate. So the best approach now is education. The reduced incidence of infection in EU or US is largely due to public awareness. However, in Africa it is really difficult. The population is growing. Some places even don't have electricity, and even more, do not believe the disease is due to the virus. How to get a clear message to people there is important. I love your idea. We might publish a short book and have a section that includes the lyrics of your "World on Fire," "A Rubber Thing," and some information about your visit to Cambodia years ago.

I reviewed an article and found that mother-to-infant transmission is lower than expected. So as long as the teens know how to protect themselves, they should be okay in normal social conditions. I did see multiple Web sites provide information about AIDS on World AIDS Day. Some were even in different languages. Don't worry too much about it. When social and economic conditions get better, more people will have better education, and more people will be fine. We as a society should try our best to send prevention messages out to as many people as possible.

Best regards,

J

The HIV pandemic is not the result of people wanting to have too much fun. It due to people having too much fun with too many partners without prevention and protection. The simplest and most effective way is using a "rubber thing," or a condom. For people in poor areas and youth, they may not have enough information or education. Education is paramount for prevention. Once people there want to protect themselves, the second issue is who should provide condoms. This is a problem in places like Africa or Cambodia. Which country should take up the challenge of shipping condoms there for free: the EU, the United States, India, or China? The best approach might be to build factories there with international funds from multiple countries. It is good to help people help themselves. In my opinion, all countries are willing to do that.

One day, Sarah posted a slogan: "Make him fall for you, and the secret Psychiatry hooked him for long time."

I commented,

Only falling for each other and being hooked for the rest of life is the classical style of living. Believe it or not, no prevention is the best prevention in the classical living style. No need for vaccine. No need for antiviral drug treatment (a lifelong one). But you do need music and songs no matter what living style you have. Sarah, I need your music. Certainly, all the fans need your music as well.

White Christmas of 2009

On December 20, 2009, there was a heavy snowfall, around 18 inches in some places, on the East Coast. After the snowfall there were sunny days, but the temperature remained below 35°F. Most of the snow had melted by December 26, 2009.

2009 Heavy Snow

It is snowing so hard, Day and Night
The earth is covered with a silver blanket
Cold and Quiet
In this freezing winter season
Christmas cactus is blooming
Fresh Red and Pink
Bring hope and life to the holidays
I'll remember you, beautiful and lovely
Warm my heart in the blizzard
Blessing my world with happiness and joy

A special thank you from fans to Sarah
Wish you have a happy and joyful holiday season!

Special Comments

Due to technical reasons, I did not go on her Web site for almost two days (Saturday and Sunday). After logging in

Monday morning, a comment was waiting for me. The comment came in Monday at about 5 a.m. EST:

> @user96098: I think you've got it bad. There's nothing wrong with having a crush on someone … sometimes, as in this case, it's a little hopeless because it can never happen in real life; it's just a fantasy. Be sure you don't let that fantasy take control of you and hurt you and cause you to do something to hurt back. You seem like such a sweet, caring, creative person and there is someone out there just hoping and praying for you to come along. There is, you know? Be patient and try not to pine away for someone you can never have. (Unless there is more to this story than the rest of us are aware of.)

I, personally, would love that! Happy holidays, J. I hope you have a wonderful, happy New Year!

> P.S. If those are your own writings, I just wanted to let you know they are beautiful … everyone of them. You have a sweet heart! Some woman would be very lucky to have you. Good luck

The next comment was:

> Sarah, I just joined today because I was surfing, looking for your song, *In the Arms of the Angels*, and when I found it, I was here. So … of course, if I joined I got to hear the new song, *One Dream*. It's a pretty song, but it'll be hard to beat *In the Arms of the Angels*. You

probably aren't trying to beat it, just putting out another good song. And that's why I'm writing this post ... to let you know *One Dream* IS a BEAUTIFUL song, too. Thank you. You have such a different, lovely voice. God has certainly blessed you and because He has blessed you, you have blessed us with your songs. Thanks again. Kaye

Well, finally someone was commenting. I was glad no matter what. I sent two e-mails to Sarah first. I thought I would just let the comments remain unanswered for a while, and then I posted the following comment:

> The first thing in medicine is "do no harm." It means to do no harm to your patients. This principle is valid in our daily life. To do no harm to others and to yourself. I am fine in that sense. Thanks a lot for your caring and nice comments. All the poems are original and I wrote them for you, Sarah. As a matter of fact, they just "came" to my heart for you. I will do my best to help and support you. It will be dream come true ... As Elvis sang, "Darling so it goes, some things are meant to be."
>
> Sarah, Happy New Year to you, and to everyone!
>
> J

This was followed by a poem:

My Angel

You care about loved ones
I'll remember you full of love
No matter to scream, weep, or be afraid of
You're the singer of my soul
These two comments posted several challenges
for me. Things are related not only to me
but also to Sarah, so I wrote the following
comment the next day as responses to the
above two comments:

Sarah, You Are Special

There are millions of great lyrics
I only have endless fun in yours
There are many great songs
Angel and One Dream are the best
There are hundreds of great singers
I only drunk in your angel voice
There are flowers all over the mountains
You are the best I love
There are thousands of beautiful girls
I am only falling for you

To celebrate New Year, I wrote "Sarah and I" for Sarah and
for everyone:

Sarah and I

You love blue
I love cyan

You play games
I play Go

You enjoy singing
I enjoy writing

You sing Silent Night
I try O, Holy Night

You have an angel voice
I was captured by voice of angel

You are so beautiful
I love all the beautiful of our world

You are the poet of our time
I love to write poems

You are in music
I am in medicine

You help the soul
I help the body

You care about AIDS epidemic
I try to find ways to prevent it

You teach youth
I want to protect teens

You worried about World On Fire
I try to bring water from ocean

Music and medicine
Body and soul
You and I

We wish peace to our world
We want to have more joy for human

Wish a Happy New Year to everyone
Wish a blooming Lilith in the Year of Tiger

On the evening of January 24, Sarah's long-expected new video "One Dream" was broadcasted on NBC. Here are some of the comments:

- The most important singer for my soul and for my heart, too. Graceful forever. New *One dream* video on NBC, Sat (Jan. 24), 8c.
- Sarah your voice surpasses that of heavenly angels who envy the purity and beauty of your gift … WOW!!!
- A beautiful movie with Olympic spirit. The best angel song and an amazing movie for the perfect fusion between music and Olympic sports, a great piece of music and Olympic history. Sarah, you are an angel of piano too.

On January 28, 2010, I posted a comment to celebrate her birthday. There were many fans celebrating her birthday on MySpace as well.

Happy 28

It was Jan 28
A special day
An angel was born
Has blessed us with angel songs since
Brought happy and joy to everyone
In this glory day
All want to sing happy BD to you
We celebrate 28th BD for you today
We will celebrate 28th BD for you next year
We will celebrate 28th BD for you every year
You are always 28
Always bring happy and joy to everyone

A 28 Heart was posted by a big fan on www.
myspace.com/sarahmclachlan

```
_____8888888888_____
_____88888888888888_____
__888888822222228888_____
_8888882222222288888_____
888888222222222288888822228888_____
8888822222222222228822222222888____
8888822222222222222222222222222288__
_88888222222222222222222222222222_88_
__88888222222222222222222222222222___888
___8888222222222222222222222222222____888
____88882222222222222222222222222_____888
_____888822222222222222222222_____888_
_____88822222222222222222_____8888__
_____888822222222222_____888888__
_____8888882222_____88888888____
_____888888_____888888888_____
_____88888888888888_____
_____888888888_____
```

On Friday, February 5, 2010, a blizzard brought at least two feet snow to the East Coast. The blizzard lasted two days. I wrote a poem about the Blizzard of 2010:

2010 Blizzard

Gray glass-like sky
Snow flakes dancing in the air
Accumulated 2" per hour for almost 2 days
TV and Computer were silent
No light, no water
A power dependent modern
Wood fire
The sign of life
Brought warm and light to human

Wood-fire boiled snow tea so enjoyful
Snow duck soup of hand-made noodle
Hot and tasty
Snow face messaging
Cold and hot
Full of fresh sensation

Dedicated workers
Big snow removing machines
Roads soon back in traffic
Power was returned to houses
Brought light, heat, and water to home

Dawn was coming
Bright sunshine over the horizon
Beautiful silver trees
On pure white snow blanket

The earth was reborn
Full of pureness and grace

Have a cup of red wine
Listen to Sarah's angel songs
Life is more appreciated and wonderful
After the hardship of Blizzard

On February 10, it was reported that McLachlan, Bryan Adams, and Rush would be among the artists expected at the opening ceremonies of the 2010 Vancouver Winter Olympic Games, according to The Canadian Press. So I wrote a poem for her:

Sarah and Winter Olympic Games

One dream
The best of angel songs
Not just an excellent music video
It's a brilliant fusion
Between music and sports
Bring courage
Not only to Sarah fans
But to all athletes
And to Olympic games
Sarah
Goes to millions
Or even billions more homes
Brings happiness
To everyone
Wish peace and joy
To the whole world

Sarah
Music superstar
Olympic super music star
International superstar
Of music and sports
A new page
Of music and Olympic Games

Sarah
You're the angel
Of music
You're the angel
Of Olympic Games

On February 12, Sarah gave an awesome performance of her song "Ordinary Miracle" in the Winter Olympic Opening Ceremonies. The Opening Ceremonies were wonderful. The province of British Columbia was a great host.

Top Music Lists

RIAA awards for albums:
- Gold: more than half a million albums sold
- Platinum: more than a million albums sold
- Diamond: more than 10 million albums sold

Based on information from the RIAA Web site and other Web sites, the current lists for best selling artists are as following:

Top 10 Best Selling Male Artists

1. BEATLES, THE
2. BROOKS, GARTH

3. PRESLEY, ELVIS
4. LED ZEPPELIN
5. EAGLES
6. JOEL, BILLY
7. AC/DC
8. JOHN, ELTON
9. JACKSON, MICHAEL
10. STRAIT, GEORGE

Top 4 Best Music Selling Female Artists
1. DION, CELINE
2. STREISAND, BARBRA
3. McLACHLAN, SARAH
4. DIXIE CHICKS

Sarah McLachlan on the Web

There is a lot of information about Sarah McLachlan on the Web. Check it out. Here are some useful links.

- www.SarahMcLachlan.com
- www.myspace.com/sarahmclachlan
- www.lilithfair.com
- www.sjmedmusic.com
- Wikipedia. "Sarah McLachlan,"
- http://en.wikipedia.org/wiki/Sarah_McLachlan
- Sarah McLachlan at the Internet Movie Database
- Sarah McLachlan's Order of Canada Citation – Governor General of Canada Website
- Sarah McLachlan Music Outreach – SMMO her inner-city youth program
- The Official World on Fire Site — with a complete list of donation recipients

- Exclusive: Sarah McLachlan at AOL Canada Music Sessions

Sarah McLachlan Discography

Available at www.sarahmclachlan.com:

1. A Life of Music
2. Acoustic Pleasures
3. Afterglow
4. Afterglow Live
5. Bloom: Remix Album
6. Closer: The Best of Sarah McLachlan
7. Disney's Greatest Hits (Disc 1)
8. Fallen
9. Fumbling towards Ecstasy
10. Live EP
11. Live From Etown: 2006 Christmas Special
12. Mirrorball
13. Mirrorball: The Complete Concert
14. Rarities, B-Sides, and Other Stuff
15. Rarities, B-Sides, and Other Stuff, Volume 2
16. Remixed
17. Solace
18. Surfacing
19. The Freedom Sessions
20. Touch
21. Video Collection 1989–1998
22. Wintersong

List of Sarah McLachlan Songs

Available at www.sarahmclachlan.com and on Sarah McLachlan's lyrics Web site:

1. Adia
2. An Inside
3. Look Angel
4. Angel with Emmylou Harris
5. Answer
6. As the End Draws Near
7. Back Door Man
8. Ben's Song
9. Blackbird
10. Black and White
11. Blue
12. Building a Mystery
13. Christmas Time Is Here
14. Circle
15. Dear God
16. Dirty Little Secret
17. Do What You Have to Do
18. Don't Give Up on Us
19. Don't Let Go (with Bryan Adams)
20. Drawn to the Rhythm
21. Drifting
22. Elsewhere
23. Fallen
24. Fear
25. Fumbling towards Ecstasy
26. Good Enough
27. Happy Xmas (War Is Over)
28. Have Yourself a Merry Little Christmas
29. Home
30. Homeless (with Ladysmith Black Mambazo)
31. Hold On

32. Hold On (Alternate Version)
33. I Love You
34. I Will Be Home for Christmas
35. I Will Remember You
36. Ice
37. Ice (Live Studio)
38. Ice Cream
39. In the Bleak Mid-Winter
40. Into the Fire
41. Just Like Me (with DMC)
42. Last Dance
43. Mary
44. Mary (Live Studio)
45. Mercy
46. O Little Town of Bethlehem
47. Ol' 55
48. One Dream
49. O Little Town of Bethlehem
50. Ordinary Miracle
51. Out of the Shadows
52. Path of Thorns
53. Perfect Girl
54. Pill with the Perishers
55. Possession
56. Possession (Piano Version)
57. Prayer of St. Francis
58. Push
59. River
60. Sad Clown
61. Silent Night
62. Silence with Delirium
63. Song for a Winter's Night

64. Steaming
65. Stupid
66. Sweet Surrender
67. The First Noel/Mary Mary
68. The Path of Thorns (Terms)
69. The Rainbow Connection
70. Time
71. Time After Time
72. Time After Time (with Cyndi Lauper)
73. Train Wreck
74. U Want Me 2
75. Unchained Melody
76. Vox
77. Wait
78. What Child Is This? (Greensleeves)
79. When She Loved Me
80. Wintersong
81. Witness
82. World On Fire

List of Sarah McLachlan Videos

Organized based on available information on www.myspace.com/sarahmclachlan:

1. A Life of Music
2. Adia (Live)
3. Adia (Acoustic)
4. Angel (look for all 6 versions)
5. Answer
6. Ben's Song
7. Big Yellow Taxi
8. Blackbird
9. Building a Mystery
10. Dirty Little Secret
11. Drawn to the Rhythm
12. Elsewhere
13. Fallen
14. Fumbling towards Ecstasy
15. Good Enough
16. Happy Xmas (War Is Over)
17. Hold On (The Freedom Sessions)
18. I Love You
19. I Love You (Live)
20. I Will Remember You
21. In the Arms of a Angel
22. Into the Fire
23. Mary
24. One Dream
25. Perfect Girl
26. Possession
27. River
28. Solsbury Hill

29. Steaming
30. Stupid
31. Sweet Surrender (Tiesto Mix)
32. The First Noel Mary Mary (Irygirl Remix)
33. The first Noel/Mary Mary (Dash Berlin)
34. The Path of Thorns (Terms)
35. Train Wreck
36. When Somebody Loved Me
37. Vox
38. World On Fire
39. World On Fire (Solarstone Afterhours Mix)

Chapter 3: Lilith Fair Tour

The Lilith Fair is a product of Sarah's creative genius. The concept was given a test run, in which McLachlan appeared in a couple of concerts with a few female artists that shared her vision. Its success brought forth the first Lilith Fair concert on September 14, 1996, in Vancouver, British Columbia.

In 1997, Sarah founded Lilith Fair tour. Sarah and other artists toured city by city for about three years. It is estimated that more than 2 million people attended Lilith Fair. Millions were contributed to charities during the tour. It was the most successful all-female music festival in human history, and one of the biggest music festivals of the 1990s. During that time Sarah and Lilith Fair were everywhere. Lilith Fair helped launch the careers of several well-known female artists. A tour consisting of all women musicians, it was called "Breast Fest" by some.

On January 28, 2009, Sarah's birthday, Carla, a fan of Sarah, posted a comment on the Web: "Back into the Loving Arms of Sarah." In that comment Carla recalled her memory of Lilith Fair. Carla commented that Sarah was a pioneer. Some people told her that something couldn't be done, but

Sarah went and did it. Amazingly, not only did she do it, but she *did it up*!

Carla recalled that all the promoters told Sarah it was not possible to have a successful all-female music tour. However, the tour enjoyed three sold-out years. Lilith Fair sent a clear message to the world that women *do* matter in rock and roll!

Carla could barely express how unbelievably stoked she was when Sarah McLachlan joined Carla and others on Ships and Dip. Sarah dared to be different and she blazed a most certain path. Carla stated that she cannot wait to set sail with Sarah on Ships and Dip!

Responses to ""Back into the Loving Arms of Sarah""

Christine Says:
March 17th, 2009 at 6:59 am

I loved her on SnD! Her concerts were beautiful and a rare occasion for us Europeans.
Thanks for having her on the boat!

News from lilithfair.com

Here are some news headlines from Lilithfair.com

Is Lilith Fair Coming to a Stage Near You?
Lilith Fair Returns, and MTV News Was There the First Time Around
—28 October 2009

Lilith Fair to Feature Mary J. Blige, Colbie Caillat, Jill Scott, More

—10 December 2009

Lilith Fair Returns with Lineup of Familiar Faces

It stated that founder Sarah McLachlan will anchor the bill, which also features Mary J. Blige, Sheryl Crow, Colbie Caillat, Erykah Badu, Tegan and Sara, and Ke$ha.

—10 December 2009

Mary J. Blige, Sheryl Crow, Sugarland, Erykah Badu Lined Up for Lilith Fair

—10 December 2009

ABC Loves Lilith

by Josef Adalian

It reported that ABC Entertainment has signed a multiplatform deal to cross-promote the upcoming revival of Lilith Fair. As part of the arrangement, ABC will hype Lilith on its shows and via the online ABC Music Lounge.

Lilith Tour 2010

First round of cities:

- Atlanta, GA
- Boston, MA
- Calgary, AB
- Chicago, IL
- Dallas, TX
- Denver, CO
- Los Angeles, CA
- Minneapolis, MN
- Montreal, QC
- New York, NY

- Philadelphia, PA
- Portland, OR
- Seattle, WA
- San Francisco, CA
- Toronto, ON
- Vancouver, BC
- Washington, DC
- London, UK

First round of artists confirmed for Lilith 2010:

- A Fine Frenzy
- Ann Atomic
- Ash Koley
- Brandi Carlile
- Butterfly Boucher
- Chairlift
- Chantal Kreviazuk
- Colbie Caillat
- Corinne Bailey Rae
- Donna De Lory
- Emmylou Harris
- Erykah Badu
- Grace Potter And The Nocturnals
- Ima
- Indigo Girls
- Ingrid Michaelson
- Janelle Monae
- Jennifer Knapp
- Jill Hennessy
- Jill Scott
- Katzenjammer

- Ke$ha
- Mary J. Blige
- Meaghan Smith
- Metric
- Miranda Lambert
- Nneka
- Sara Bareilles
- Sarah McLachlan
- Serena Ryder
- Sheryl Crow
- The Submarines
- Sugarland
- Tara MacLean
- Tegan And Sara
- Vedera
- The Weepies
- Vita Chambers
- Ximena Sarinana
- Zee Avi

New cities were announced on January 21, 2010. Fifteen additional cities have been revealed, with more to come in the next few weeks:

- Austin
- Charlotte
- Detroit
- Edmonton
- Hartford
- Houston
- Indianapolis
- Nashville

- Phoenix
- Raleigh
- San Diego
- Salt Lake City
- St. Louis
- Tampa
- West Palm Beach

New artists have also been added to the tour:

- Heart
- Norah Jones
- Cat Power
- Sia
- Gossip
- La Roux
- Ceci Bastida
- Erin McCarley
- Frazey Ford
- Julia Othmer
- Kate Nash
- Lights
- Missy Higgins
- Lissie
- Marina & The Diamonds
- Pricilla Renea
- Rosie Thomas
- Toby Lightman
- Melissa McClelland
- Beth Orton
- Elizaveta

A Blooming Garden

An evergreen garden
Full of blooming plants
Roses of Angel
Jasmine of Cowboys
Holiday Cactus of Firecracker
The best flowers since 1997

It is the 2nd season
Bright sunshine
Fresh water
Love of Sarah
Blossom'll soon back in NA
Lilith, the garden of our time

Chapter 4: Music, Sarah, Medicine, and Human Health

Human Health

Human health can be divided into the health of the body and the health of the soul or physical health and mental health. Medicine, through the hard and dedicated work of medical professionals, played and plays significant role in the health of our body. Many drugs have been developed and approved and are effective in the control and treatment of many diseases, such as antibiotics, insulin, antiviral drugs, replacement enzymes, and so on. Prevention medicine plays more and more role in our life. Current vaccines have prevented the occurrence of many deadly infectious diseases and significantly improved our life. Behavioral science is part of medicine, which in a way deals with the health of our soul, and a lot more needed to be done in this field. The role of music in the health of our soul is an interesting new topic and there are a lot more need to be discussed and done. Based on the novel data that will be presented in this chapter, it has been found that Sarah's songs have played an important role in the lives of many people, not only fans, making them happy during difficult times, helping them overcome the mental challenges that they were facing, and even saving a depressed person.

The intent of this book is not to lecture in medicine. There are many excellent medical books out there. Please find one that suits your needs.

Medicine is everywhere in our life. From childhood to old age, we all need medicine in a way. Some human beings are even created with the assistance of medical professionals. Bringing high quality health care to the public is not an easy job. It is not only the doctors and other professionals that need to be trained over long periods to ensure they provide the best care possible in a timely manner, but also academics, FDA, and health professionals require many years to discover, develop, manufacture, examine, and review these products to ensure that only safe and effective products will be released to the market to enhance public health.

Alternative medicine provides some additional care and is beneficial in some ways. Whether music should be included as a therapy is an interesting subject. We are going to explore the therapeutic value of music based on preliminary but novel data that we have. Whether medical school should have a music department is a subject for future discussion.

The major diseases that affect human health are discussed briefly below. The role of music in the life of people suffering these diseases is explored briefly.

Infectious Diseases

The discovery of antibiotics and the development of vaccines have significantly reduced the mobility of and mortality caused by microbes. The development and marketing of effective preventive vaccine and anti-microbe drugs is one of the major advancements of medical science. However, severe microbe infections (including sepsis and septic shock) remain major healthcare problems (affecting millions of individuals each year) and drug-resistant microbes are constant emerging that put significant pressure on current antibiotics.

Microbes are foreign organisms. Ideally, effective vaccines should be developed to induce lifelong immunity. Despite intense efforts in the past, there are huge hurdles that are dealing or preventing the development of effective vaccines for many microbes, especially bacteria. It is paramount to improve the effectiveness of current available vaccine candidates.

Cancer

Cancer is the second leading cause of death in United States. It is quite different from infectious diseases. For some infectious diseases, such as HIV-1, prevention could play a significant role in the control of the disease. However, there are so many uncertainties when dealing with cancer. A lot has been done in the field of cancer research. Now we have plenty information about the diseases—such as genetic defects or mutations, oncogenes, tumor suppressor genes, tumor immunology, the role of chemokines in the migration or metastasis of cancer cells, tumor stem cells, and the impact of environment (like smoking) on tumor development. A tumor vaccine has recently been approved by FDA that is effective in the control of cervical cancer. But a lot more needs to be done. It is a simple fact that despite the advances, the number of cancer-caused deaths has not fallen much.

Breast Cancer

Because the Lilith Fair tour consists entirely of females (and was even referred to as the "Breast Fest" by some), I would like to talk a little bit more about breast cancer.

Breast cancer is quite different from other solid tumors. Patients may survive more than twenty or thirty years after surgical removal of breast cancer. Early diagnosis is very important. Due to the fact that the locations of the cancer are usually superficial, early diagnosis is possible. Therefore, breast cancer screening is a must. Current guidelines for the screening are as follow:

The new breast cancer screening guidelines from the US Preventive Services Task Force (USPSTF) were published in the November 17, 2009, issue of the *Annals of Internal Medicine*. The guidelines were based on the efficacy of film mammography, CBE, BSE, digital mammography, and MRI, in lowering breast cancer mortality rates.

- The USPSTF recommends against routine screening mammography in women aged 40 to 49 years.
- Women aged 50 to 74 years should undergo biennial screening mammography.
- The additional benefits and harms of CBE beyond screening mammography in women 40 years or older is insufficient to determine.
- Additional benefits and harms of either digital mammography or MRI vs. film mammography as screening modalities for breast cancer is insufficient to determine at this time.

In my opinion, it is not a bad idea to perform a self-check or have your partner carefully check it for you several times a year, especially if you are not in a high-risk group and do not plan to have mammography screening done when over forty. Mammography, as well as physical examination of the breasts, can detect pre-symptomatic breast cancer. If you are aged forty to forty-nine and are concerned you are high risk, please discuss with your doctor to determine whether and when you should start mammography screening. Due to the possibility of false positives, you should have a second opinion on whether you have cancer and whether you should have a mastectomy done.

Cardiovascular Diseases

Cardiovascular disease is the leading cause of death in the United States. Diet and living habits play significant roles in the control of the disease. Healthy food, such as one low in fat, high in fruits and vegetables, and moderate in meat consumption, could significantly delay or prevent the development of the disease. Moderate exercise each day (30 minutes a day) will maintain our overall body health and may even provide a spiritual high. If you care, you could reduce your risk of having cardiovascular disease. The dramatic reduction in incidence of cardiac deaths in recent years indicates that we do care.

Diabetes

It was estimated that at least 171 million people worldwide suffer from diabetes (or 2.8 percent of the population). Thank God we have had insulin for years. Currently the best care for insulin-dependent diabetes (or type I diabetes) is to tightly control the blood sugar level, thereby delaying or preventing the incidence of complications that might be life threatening otherwise. Due to immune rejection and ethical issues, a blood sugar level sensitive mechanic, rather than a biologic, pump that can self-adjust the output of insulin in a pattern mimic human pancreas might provide additional benefits to patient in the control of blood sugar level.

Depression

About 3.5 percent of people might experience depression during their lifetime. There are effective and safe drugs available for treatment. Get physician care and treatment early if you do experience a really low mood for weeks that begins to affect your daily work and life.

Low mood for a couple of days may result from the loss of a significant other, unhappiness at work, or a recent birth. You might get better as time goes on. Activities like talking to friends, going to parties, or doing some exercise might help. Another thing that you can try, based on current information, is to listen to music—either at a concert, on the radio, or even just singing to yourself. Different music may have a different effect on different people, so select the music that makes *you* feel better. You can try Sarah McLachlan or other artists. It is unknown at this time whether people respond better to singers of their own gender or the opposite gender.

Music and Happiness

Here I present two comments posted on the "One Dream" Facebook page:

Comment A

Music and Happiness

Beautiful music and beautiful voice. It is so great and I can't help to introduce a series of short discussions about music in our life. Thanksgiving is a big holiday for many people each year. Families get together, eat delicious food, talk to each other, then many will turn on music. Even more, some will sing, others will dance with music. There are many great holiday songs, like "Happy Xmas—Wintersong." Really to me, holidays without friends, family members, relatives, and music would not be a happy holiday.

Comment B

Well, many things are important to humans. We need air, water, food and we need friends, family, etc. One thing, among others, that is essential to me is listening to music, especially Sarah's beautiful songs. Many fans have the same feelings. When they drive along, when they feel sad and unhappy, it is Sarah's songs with them. Believe it or not, magic is magic.

PBS young@heart

The role of music in lives of people was observed in PBS's young@heart. This special program reported that we can see how music, especially music performed live, helped seniors maintain a high quality of spiritual life, helps them connect with others, and more importantly helped them fight diseases, such as heart disease and cancer. How that happened is a very interesting topic that needs to be explored further, but one thing is clear: these performances kept them not only feeling happy but also physically active, therefore contributing to the better medical outcomes.

Music and Hardships

People say
We'll sing

When happy
We'll sing
When with friends
We'll sing
During holidays

I'll ask
Will you sing
Before a danger battle?
Will you sing
When sad?
Will you sing
When not happy?
Will you sing
During hardship?

The answer is
Why not?
Believe it or not
Singing will encourage
Fighters to win
Singing will help
Overcome sadness
Singing will lift
Unhappiness
Singing will help
Leading you
Out of hardship

And equally important
Singing will help
Leading others

To a better mood
To overcome
Difficult situations
So why not

Sing, sing, sing, Sarah
At this special Valentine 's Day
Wish you
Have a very successful tour
And keep singing for another 20 or 30 years
Like the best of last night
Performed by you
Bring joy to the Opening Ceremony
Bring happiness to every audience

To celebrate Valentine's Day and Chinese New
Year, I wrote a poem:

Valentine New Year

Valentine's sunshine
Bright and warm
New Year silver blanket
Shining and cold
Night dreams
Rich and exciting
Day reality
Full of caring and grace
Dream and reality
Reality and dream
All happy parts of life

In the New Year Valentine's Day
Make a wish, Sarah
Dream will be true

In the Valentine New Year
Make a wish, my friends
Sarah will be with us every day

Sarah's Songs and Public Health

We know now that music definitely cannot cure cancer or diabetes. However, can music make people feel better in normal or low mood?

The role of music in human happiness was introduced to Sarah's Facebook page in November 2009. The role of music in human health was suggested by a reported at one Website. During the 1990s, there were a few female singer-songwriters who blazed a trail for the female movement, one of them being Canadian Grammy award winner Sarah McLachlan. Her emotional ballads have become her trademark sound, and another claim to fame is that she founded Lilith Fair, the most successful all female music festival in history.

One of her most famous songs has become a timeless classic since it was released ten years ago. With just Sarah at the piano, "Angel" is one of those songs that you can't help but like. Singer DMC from the rap group Run-DMC has credited this song with saving his life. Although we do not know what happened exactly, his claim suggests that *Angel* might have changed his mind in a way that kept him alive and happier.

The following report about the above event was found on Wikipedia:

In 2004, Darryl "D.M.C." McDaniels, who credits McLachlan and her music for lifting him from a period of depression, invited her to join him on a track from his solo album. Although the album was not released until early 2006, remixes of the song *Just Like Me* were included on a number of compilations in 2005.

Comments from Sarah's One Dream Site on Facebook

More findings on Sarah's Facebook page support the role of music in public health. Here are some of the comments:

Beautiful song, beautiful voice, beautiful lady

- Simply sublime
- Cool song
- Just perfect
- Beautiful new song Sarah!
- Great song, amazing voice
- Beautiful voice, beautiful woman, beautiful sentiment!!!
- Fab voice Sarah
- Sarah sings with a voice of angel
- The most amazing voice I've ever heard!
- This is an amazing song. She is the best.
- You have never ceased to amazing my ears and my heart!
- A beautiful song performed to perfection by this beautiful lady
- You have the most beautiful voice, your lyrics go deep into the heart and soul.
- You have a face of angel and the voice of one too.

- The most important singer for my soul and my heart. Full of grace forever!

Inspiration

- You've an inspiration to so many, keep it up!
- You've been such an inspiration to me.
- Sarah sings like no other! She places us in the arms of angels and inspires us by the beauty and humanity of her voice and spirit!

Bring happiness, overcome sadness

- Very comforting and warm.
- I am so excited.
- History will record the spirit of your music, and the spirit you have used to bring happiness to others.
- I always await her next release with happiness.
- I was saddened when you left the scene for a bit.
- Your music has helped so many of us during the difficult times. You have definitely touched my soul and helped me through some sad times.
- Your music has helped me out so much in my life that I feel that it has gotten me through some really hard times.
- I take your music on long trips, during long drives on lonely highways … and knowing the comfort that your voice is there to keep me company. Just like last week, while my father passed away and I was traveling, you were there to keep me going, and focus on where I need to be.

From these comments, one can clearly see that for most people her songs are beautiful, lovely, amazing, fab, bliss, wonderful, and so on. Many were attracted by her beautiful voice. In short, people feel that her songs are really pleasant to listen to and feel more satisfied after listening to them. To others that were going through difficult times, in a low mood, or just lonely, her songs have provided companionship and support to overcome the difficult situations that they were facing. In some extreme cases they may have even saved lives. Her songs make people with depression feel better even if they are not on antidepressants. In short, her music cannot hurt. In summary, Sarah's songs make people feel happy, lift low mood, and even make depressed people feel better too. Only you can determine whether it is good for you, so why not try it out?

My Angel

You care about the youth
Happy Xmas singing alone with girls and boys
No matter elementary, middle, or high
You are the musician of my mind

You care about friends
ADIA expressing rich color of life
No matter feeling empty, faltering, or innocent
You're the artist of my mind

You care about loved ones
I'll remember you full of love
No matter to scream, weep, or be afraid of
You're the poet of my heart

You care about human
One dream a dream for everyone
No matter black, white, or yellow
You are the singer of my soul

You care about the world
World on fire revealing a big and tender heart
No matter Africa, America, or Europe
You are the angel of my heart

One Dream Letters to Sarah

A letter regarding *One Dream*:

December 17, 2009

Dear Sarah,

You will not be alone. I will always be with you. To me, there are two things essential to you and me: the world and human wellness. You have passion for the world. You care about it. "World On Fire" is the best song, as it revealed your passion. Your passion is my passion too. I am sucked to you by your songs and by your passion. Now your happiness is every fan's happiness. I am determined to encourage you, to support you to accomplish your goals to make people feel better, to overcome sadness and difficult moments. Your happiness is one of the most important things to all fans. I have a lot of courage for you, and for humanity. I can carry history, a lot of it, because I ususally do not let the downside of history drag too much. If I have to consider history, it will just try to avoid similar mistakes to happen today or tomorrow. Talk to you later.

Best wishes,

J

***

December 19, 2009

Sarah, My Dear,

I like to play. I have played many different games, Chinese Chess, Chess, Go, bridge. I like dancing too. One day I hope I will dance with you. Get ready, I am going to dance with you all night. The only game that I was really sucked into was Go, a game popular in China, Taiwan, Japan, and Korea. I am fine with gambling. I did it several times, but I am not really into it. I only smoke when I drive in the middle of the night, like 1 or 2 a.m., when my Coke does not work anymore. One pack for me could last for one or two years. Normally I do not drink, although I like to have a little bit of beer sometimes. Now my hobby is to listen to music, to watch your music videos, and to support you. Sometimes I try to sing a little myself. When I have chance, I will be happy to play games with you anytime you want and we will have a lot of fun. Because to you music is a professional thing, it is good to have something away from music for you. Don't think, don't listen, and don't watch MUSIC. Gardening is fun for summer. Talking to plants, watching flowers, and picking tomato are fun things to do. Fishing, swimming, and boating are all fun too. I can play Go with you. Go is an easy game. You will know how to play it in minutes, because you are so smart. We then can play a 9 x 9 Go game if you are interested. I am pretty good at teaching (brag). You can teach me your favorite games.

Talk to you later.

Best,

J

Forever Love

There are many kinds of love. Love songs explore human feeling of all kinds connecting loved ones together. Love songs are forever. The following are the different types of human love:

People lovers: I knew a pastor since 1990. As a pastor, his job demanded that he help others, his brothers and sisters. But more importantly, he wanted to help others. He really did his best to help others and to spread the messages of

God that he truly believed, through music and through his actions. Five years ago, when he was diagnosed with end-stage nasopharyngeal carcinoma, everyone in the church tried their best to help him. I am not a church member, but based on my experience I suggested that he should consider surgery in Hong Kong. He had surgery and fought the cancer for five more years. This is an example of forever love—everyone wanted to help a helper, to love a lover of life.

Family love: This is the love of children, parents, brothers, and sisters. Just a phone call or a few days together can show others that you are connected. Don't weep for the occasional disappointments; we are still a big family. This kind of love is forever.

Friend love: You can see that in Sarah's life. Her lifelong friendship with Pierre Marchand, though it began with romantic love, is still a fruitful one. "ADIA" is a song with a strong attempt to save friendship with Crystal Heald, a girlfriend of Sarah. They are still very good girlfriends, as Sarah said, levelers of life. As so it goes, some things are meant to be. Those are examples of friend love. It is strong and forever filled with goodwill.

Colorful love: The love between two partners in love might be the one with the most color and exclusiveness. It is the most personal and the strongest, and it makes people feel beautiful and strong. It could make one sleep less, filling their dreams with the object of their desire. It can make one full of energy, full of desire to get things done, more creative, smarter, and so on. You want to be closer and to make your loved one happy. If it is all right, you want her to want U 2, you need her to need U 2, you love her to love U 2. You consider her a lot. You have common goals for man and our world. You both just want to be together forever. You care each other. You worry about each other. There are many great testimonies of this type of love. The words of Andy in *Love Story* say it well: "When I reach for her hand, it's always there." Or as Sarah sings in *Good Enough*, "I'll be there for you." These are both beautiful expressions of this type of love.

Sarah's "World On Fire" and Josh Groban's "You Raise Me High" represent another kind of love, a love of our country and our world, an endless and forever love.

The following poem is for all the lovely couples in the world and all the singles that are looking for love. I wish all of you have your colorful love forever and care for each other forever.

Forever Love

You came to my life
When I heard your angel voice the first time
Beautiful angel voice so special
Can't help to listen to you forever

You came to my dream
When I saw you the first time
Beautiful you are so lovely
Wish you happy and beautiful forever

U want me 2
Brought in deep sadness and irresistible beauty
You're so beautiful and so lovely

Just want you happy forever

You came to my dream
When colorful you 1st into my eyes
When we're together morning and night
Beautiful poems
Angel songs
Great passions
Gentle and tender heart
One dream
Drawn us together forever
There for each other
Care youth
Love our world
Wish forever peace and joy to everyone

You are the tree of my life
Forever green on the mountains and in the
valley
Care the body
Care the soul
Care each other forever
Our soul
Fused as one
No more waiting
No more hesitating
Forever love is coming

We fused as one
No air in between
No space in between
Love happily, love dearly, love deeply forever

Our love is strong and for lifetime
Forever life and forever love are coming
Our life and our love are forever

One day Sarah provided a poetry publishing site. Now I am writing this book with many poems to explore music in life and wish you will find out the best music for yourself, and for improving your life and the life of your loved ones.

Chapter 5: Questions and Answers

1. **Q: Does music have medical value?**

   A: Although it has been reported in Wikipedia that music therapy has been used in the treatment of a few diseases in psychiatry, our focus here is different. Our goal is to assess whether it can make normal happier, lift low mood, and make depressed people feel normal. Although the data that we have is preliminary, it suggests that music makes people happier. Therefore, the contribution of music to wellness and public health is evident. As we discussed previously, the comments posted on Sarah's Facebook page indeed suggest that her music can provide support, relaxation, and fun to those in a low mood because of depression or some traumatic event. The data we presented here suggest that everyone could benefit from his or her own favorite music or songs. Of course, when you have severe medical conditions or you feel you need to you should seek medical care as soon as possible.

2. **Q: Do songs do the same thing?**

A: Due to our different culture backgrounds, the impact of a certain type of music may vary from one individual to another. Even individuals with similar cultural backgrounds might make quite different musical selections. There are social and economic limitations as well. But one thing is clear: great music and voices can cross the barriers of languages, societies, and cultures.

3. **Q: Do all people respond to the same music the same way?**

A: Although many people might not have preference of a special singer, usually the fans for one singer might not be fans for another singer. The various responses between males and females to a given singer is also interesting. For love songs, females might more keen to male voices. On the other hand, males might prefer to listen to female voices. Because people have the desire to express themselves so they might more like to listen to the same sex singers so they can follow in that respect. It is worth mentioning that both males and females love Sarah's songs, an angel's voice loved by all individuals.

4. Q: How can I find the music best for me?

A: There are many ways you can find the music best for you. Young people in this country are fortunate to be exposed to all kinds of music during their school years—either in chorus, in band, or in concerts. Listening to the radio is another way. Find a radio station near you or through the Internet. A third way to learn about new singers is through books. In this book we have provided information about a great singer of our time—her biography, her lists of beautiful songs, videos, and albums, so that you can listen to her songs and download your favorite ones onto your MP3 player from Amazon or iTunes. More importantly, we have observed the fact that Sarah's songs made people happier. Perhaps they will make you happier in your trying situations, so we share this information with you here.

5. Q: How to control the spread of HIV?

A: The first thing to know is that disease is transmitted from person to person. Education, and especially education for teens, is paramount. Being in a long-term committed relationship between partners is the best natural prevention. If not, wearing a condom is a must, or you may have to take antiviral drugs for the rest of your life. In poor areas, like Africa, education and access to condoms are paramount. Social and economic improvements in those areas will help a lot.

6. Q: Can cancer be cured?

A: While cancer is not yet curable, it is at least preventable, by avoiding things such as smoking, industry pollution, food contamination, and certain viral infections. The cancer vaccine for PVP is a good start for women. Controlling industrial pollution is not only a key to controlling climate change but also essential to maintaining the health of humans on this globe. There are no "firewalls" to floating industry dust—they merely float from one place to another. Water contamination is often seen locally, resulting in "cancer villages" in some countries.

The fight against cancer might be one of the greatest challenges in human history. Many have fought for the cure and are fighting still. With the sequencing of entire human genome, as well as advancements in molecular biology, cell biology, immunology, and the manufacturing of equipment like confocal microscopes, special targeting systems, and delivery systems, we will get there one day.

One of the key questions in fighting cancer is what to target: the cell surface, the cytoplasm, or the nuclear?

7. Q: How do I reach a happy hundredth birthday?

A: It has been reported that individuals can reach 122 years with a good mental status. Eternal life might be part of our future, but this will likely take even longer than the fight against cancer. People reaching their hundredth birthdays might be a first reachable step. We know we can't choose our genes, so we must be happy with what we have. But there are things can be done that will make us healthier and happier.

Here are some suggestions that will not only help you to live longer but help you live happier.

- Get 30 minutes of moderate physical activity a day. Walk, work in the garden, or do whatever you like to do physically.
- Practice good dietary habits. Don't smoke. Don't drink too much. Don't eat too much at a time. Eat more fish. Reduce fat intake. Have more fruit and vegetables.
- Establish a daily routine. Get enough sleep. Avoid drugs if possible. For retired persons, you might consider an after-lunch rest or nap. Self-message might be good.
- Maintain good social activities. Family and friends are important.
- Have routine physical checkups. Early diagnosis is the key to fighting cancer, and it makes huge difference in outcomes and survival rates. For breast cancer, it is possible to survive for twenty or even thirty years after early diagnosis and early surgery.

- Listen to music or perform music yourself. You can exercise when you are listening. Make your own music mixes, including both female singers (such as Sarah) and male singers. You may sing by yourself or together with others.

I further provided detailed information and suggestions to several recommedations of question #7 and some were posted on Sarah's One Dream Facebook:

> Happy New Year to Sarah and everyone! In the New Year and the new decade, I wish Sarah and all a great year, a great tour, a happy decade, and a wonderful life.

It has been reported that individuals can reach 122 years old with good mental status. Eternal life might be a future. But it certainly will take even longer than the fight to cancer. But, but could we have more people celebrating their 100th birthday? I think this is the first step that is reachable. There are some notable facts that will not only help you to live longer, but live happier.

We know we can't choose our genes, so we must be happy with what we have. But there are things that can be done and will make us healthier and happier.

A. 30 minutes moderate physical activity a day. Walking, working in farms, gardens, or doing what ever you like.

Lack of enough physical activity is the second leading contributor to preventable death. A sedentary lifestyle has been linked to 28 percent of mortality from leading chronic diseases.

Walking two miles or more per day is associated with nearly 50 percent lower age-related mortality in older non-smoking men. A significant difference in benefit was seen between no activity and moderate activity.

Regular moderate or vigorous exercise reduces the patient's risk of myocardial infarction, stroke, hypertension, hyperlipidemia, type 2 diabetes, and osteoporosis. Patients with chronic illness could benefit from mild to moderate exercise.

B. Good diet habit. No smoking. Don't drink too much. Don't eat too much each time. Eat more fish. Reduce fat intake. Have more fruit and vegetable.

Smoking is the leading cause of preventable death. There are between 1.1 and 1.4 billion smokers in the world out of a total population of around 5.8 billion. It has been estimated that 50 percent of smokers will die prematurely from tobacco-related illness, half in middle age (defined as 35–69 years of age) with an average loss of life expectancy of 20–25 years (8 years over all ages). Tobacco death toll hits 40 millions for decade (According to ASH, 14th World Conference on Tobacco Or Health 2009, and The Global Tobacco Epidemic 2008: WHO report). Whether we should blame the person or blame a possible "smoking gene" is debatable at this time. I tried cigarettes when I was nine with my classmates. But somehow I never really like it. Perhaps I do not have the "smoking gene." Neither my father nor my brother smokes cigarettes. One thing is clear: if you do not try it, even if you have a "smoking gene," you might be fine. For example, you might just started to smoke when you were 15 years old. You were fine for the first 15 years. The better way might be "do not try it."

Having some red wine for 4 to 5 times a week for a man (or 2 to 3 times for a woman) might be good for your cardiovascular system. But too much might cause liver problems. One may debate why the French drink more and have fewer heart diseases than the British. The active components in red wine are polyphenols, such as resveratrol, phenolic acids, anthocyanins, and flavonoids. These polyphenols have been shown to have potent activities of antioxidant, reducing LDLlevels and platelet aggregation. These compounds also possess anti-atherosclerotic and vaso-relaxationactivities.

Having a cup of green tea is not a bad idea. In 1999, the magazine *Nature* reported that green tea extracts can prevent the growth of new vessels. Drinking green tea is associated with a lower incidence of human cancer.

C. Keep good social activities. Friends and family are important.

Church is a special place for many. There are at least three things that attract so many people to church. The belief in God and the afterlife is the first reason. Second, church members are brothers and sisters—they care each other and help each other during difficult times, when sick, when lonely, or after a trauma. It is a place to talk, to communicate, to care, and to be cared for. The third reason is the church music. With more than thousand years of history and a possible origin from heaven, the melodies of many church songs are really good. Singing them at weekend services, especially during the holidays, provides comfort, relief, and hope for many. Some will forget their loneness, feeling happy and loved instead.

One important aspect of social activities is conversation. Since any sound could be music, the party voices might not be as beautiful as a symphony orchestra, but might be just doing well for you. Therefore, try to go to parties, even if you are feeling low, sad, or lonely. Find interesting local activities and be there to listen and talk.

I was told by a friend that a psychiatry nurse wondered why her patients could not take care of themselves and get out of their situations. One day she called my friend and told her that she could not sleep for many days. My friend and the pastor, who died of nasopharyngeal carcinoma, as mentioned before, went to see her. The pastor talked to her for some time and she fell asleep. Maybe it was what the pastor said, or maybe it was just his voice. We all know good songs can help babies sleep. People with sleeping problems may benefit from listening to light music, talking to loved ones, having a hot bath, or having some milk or yogurt. Remember, we sleep one third of our lives, so a good night's sleep is very important in our life.

Conclusion

Music has long been a part of human life. With advances in technology including the iPod and the Internet, music has become a part of nearly everyone's life, from infants to seniors. We know music is pleasant to listen to, but its impact on human health is a field that needs to be explored. We all know that medicine is essential to our health, but can the same be said for music? In this book, some novel data has been provided relating to music and human health, which indicates that music play an important role in human health. Two facts strongly support this conclusion. First, Sarah McLachlan, a world famous female singer and a three-time Grammy winner, who is beautiful and inspiring songs have helped many people during difficult times, has brought happiness and joy to many—even saving life. Second, the program Young@Heart, aired on PBS, highlighted the importance of music in keeping a young heart in senior chorus members with average age of eighty-one, helping them to age gracefully and even to fight diseases like cancer and heart disease.

How to have a happy and healthy life is perhaps the most important topic to everyone. There are several basic things that everyone can do to make one's life happy and healthier.

These include getting enough physical activity daily, listening to good music, maintaining a balanced diet rich in fruits and vegetables, and networking with friends and maintaining social activities. Taking care your loved ones and getting a good night's sleep are important too. If we all do these basic things, it is likely we will reduce our risk for many diseases. With the help of vaccines and good medical care, a happy, healthy, and graceful life is possible for everyone who does care.

Dear readers,

Thank you for your support.

You can find more information about Sarah McLachlan's, songs, videos, and books from the following Web sites:

www.sarahmclachlan.com

www.myspace.com/sarahmclachlan

www.sjmedmusic.com

About the Author

Jin H. Wang is a medical doctor in the DC Metro area. Jin loves scientific writing and has many scientific publications. Jin loves music and is a tenor himself. This is his first book about art and public health. Jin believes that all medical schools should have a music department in the future.

Lilith Tour Final Schedule

June 27, 8:00P
McMahon Stadium, Calgary, Alberta

June 28, 8:00P
Northlands Spectrum, Edmonton, Alberta

July 1, 8;00P
Pitt Meadows Airport, Vancouver, British Columbia

July 2 8:00P
The Amphitheatre at Clark County, Portland, Oregon

Jul 3 12:00A
The Gorge, Seattle, Washington

Jul 5 8:00P
Shoreline Amphitheatre at Mountain View, San Francisco, California

Jul 7 8;00P
Cricket Wireless Amphiteatre, San Diego, California

Jul 8 8:00P
Cricket Wireless Pavilion, Phoenix, Arizona

Jul 9 8;00P
*Mandalay Bay Events Cente*r, Las Vegas, Nevada

Jul 10 8:00P
Verizon Wireless Amphiteatre, Los Angeles

Jul 12 8:00P
USANA Amphitheatre, Salt Lake City, Utah

Jul 13 8:00P
Comfort Dental Amphitheatre, Denver, Colorado

Jul 15 8:00P
Capitol Federal Park at Sandstone, Kansas City, Missouri

Jul 16 8:00P
Verizon Wireless Amphitheater St Louis,St. Louis, Missouri

Jul 17 8:00P
First Midwest, Chicago, Illinois

Jul 18 8:00P
MN Canterbury Park, Minneapolis, Minnesota

Jul 20 8:00P
Verizon Wireless Music Center, Indianapolis, Indiana

Jul 21 8:00P
DTE Energy Music Theatre, Detroit, Michigan

Jul 23 8:00P
Parc Jean-Drapeau, Montreal, Quebec

Jul 24 8:00P
Molson Canadian Amphitheatre, Toronto, Ontario

Jul 27 8:00P
Blossom Music Center, Cleveland, Ohio

Jul 28 8:00P
Susquehanna Bank Center, Philadelphia, Pennsylvania

Jul 30 8:00P
Comcast Center, Boston, Massachusetts

Jul 31 8:00P
PNC Bank Arts Center, New York, New York

Aug 1 8:00P
Comcast Theatre, Hartford, Connecticut

Aug 3 8:00P
TBA, Washington, Washington DC

Aug 4 8:00P
Time Warner Cable Music Pavilion at Walnut Creek, Raleigh, North Carolina

Aug 6 8:00P
Verizon Wireless Amphitheatre Charlotte, Charlotte, North Carolina

Aug 7 8:00P
Bridgestone Arena, Nashville, Tennessee

Aug 8 8:00P
Aaron's Amphitheatre, Atlanta, Georgia

Aug 10 8:00P
Cruzan Amphitheatre, W. Palm Beach, Florida

Aug 11 8:00P
Ford Ampitheatre, Tampa, Florida

Aug 12 8:00P
Verizon Wireless Music Center Birmingham, Birmingham, Alabama

Aug 14 8:00P
TBA, Austin, Texas

Aug 15 8:00P
Cynthia Woods Mitchell Pavilion, Houston, Texas

Aug 16 8:00P
Superpages.com Center, Dallas, Texas

Index